To Lane

Thanks for your input!

Top Mistakes Danes Make In English

A fun guide to small but significant errors

Updated edition

Other books by Kay Xander Mellish
How to Live in Denmark
How to Work in Denmark

Published in Denmark in 2018 by KXMGroup, via Books on Demand.

Copyright © Kay Xander Mellish 2016, 2018

All rights reserved

No part of this book may be reproduced in any form or by any electronic or mechanical means, including information storage and retrieval systems, without written permission from the author, except for brief quotations in a book review.

ISBN 978-8-77-114188-7

To the people of Nykøbing Falster,
which I mistakenly called "Nykøbing Falstaff"
for my first ten years in Denmark.

Contents

Preface	9
Talking about 'my private economy'	13
Using 'both' for more than two items	15
Mixing up 'wanting' and 'wishing'	17
Leaving out the 'c' in exciting	19
Bragging about 'living in a hotel'	21
Mispronouncing 'prize' as 'price'	23
Asking about 'bringing' a news article	25
Not knowing 'obviously' is obnoxious	27
Using 'meet' to mean 'start work'	29
Translating 'eventuelt' as 'eventually'	31
Starting a sentence with 'especially'	33
Adding 'etc.' to every single list	35
Confusing 'fun' and 'funny'	37
Translating 'derfor' and 'hermed' directly	39
Saying 'I've tried' to describe unplanned experiences	41
Mixing up 'customer' and 'costumer'	43
Confusing 'learn' with 'teach' or 'loan' with 'borrow'	45
Using 'revert' in place of 'reply'	47
Thinking 'competent' is a compliment	49
Spelling 'lose' with a double 'o'	51

Repeating a full name throughout a text	53
Trying to schedule with week numbers	55
Mixing up 'personal' and 'private'	57
Using English profanity lightly	59
Thinking a 'sparring partner' is a friend	61
Confusing 'effective' and 'efficient'	63
Choosing 'possibility' instead of 'opportunity'	65
Unfortunate direct translations	67
Picking the wrong verb conjugation	69
Using 'follow' to mean 'accompany'	71
Playing on Danish modesty	73
Writing long and complex sentences	75
Misplacing apostrophes	77
Avoiding contractions	79
Using 'already' to describe a future event	81
About the author	83

Preface

Danes speak wonderful English. They begin studying it when they are barely out of diapers, and will probably hear it spoken almost every day for the rest of their lives.

Most pop music heard in Denmark is in English, and American TV shows and movies are not generally dubbed unless they are for children. A lot of Danish university classes are taught in English, and professors assign English-language papers.

When Danes travel outside of their small country — even, increasingly, when they visit Sweden and Norway — they speak English to everyone they meet.

But it is almost impossible to speak a second language perfectly, as I know from personal experience. I'm a native English speaker who has lived in Denmark for more than a decade, yet I still struggle with small challenges in Danish.

Whether I'm taking a fraction of a second to figure out if I should use **Jeg tror** or **Jeg synes** (they're both covered by *I think* in English) or mixing up **lege** and **leje** (*Would your daughter like to come over and **rent** with my daughter on Friday?*) I'm never entirely confident in Danish.

And as an occasional Danish-to-English translator, I always struggle to translate uniquely Danish words like **hyggelig**,

kæreste, døgn, and **nærværende** into English.

This little book isn't designed to make fun of Danes. In fact, Danes have a remarkable sense of humor about themselves.

It's just a quick remedy for the small mistakes Danes make so that they can bring their English skills that much closer to flawless, and feel even more comfortable speaking English.

Kay Xander Mellish
Spring 2018

Talking about 'my private economy'

An economy, in English, is a large-scale thing with many moving parts - the *Danish economy*, the *digital economy*. Occasionally, you'll hear discussion of *microeconomics* if you hang out with people who work in the aid-to-developing-nations sector.

But there's no such a thing as a private economy, at least not in commonly spoken English.

Your bank accounts, credit cards and investments make up your *personal finances* or *family budget*.

Using 'both' for more than two items

The Danish **både** can be used for a seemingly infinite list of items, but in English, *both* can be applied only to sets of two.

When used in longer lists — <u>She's an expert in both kung fu, archery and cookie-making</u> — it feels disorienting.

Just drop the word *both,* or rephrase the sentence: *She is skilled at **both** baking and fighting sports.*

Mixing up 'wanting' and 'wishing'

Every successful businessperson pays attention to what customers want, yet the Danish buzzword **kundeønsker** is frequently mistranslated as *customer wishes*.

Wants and wishes are very different in English: A *want* is something a customer has a good chance of getting, while a *wish* is lovely but unlikely.

*Customers **want** healthy sandwiches. I **wish** Prince Harry would serve me a healthy sandwich.*

Since English-speaking societies tend to be ones in which the consumer is king, I usually translate **kundeønsker** as *customer demands*.

Leaving out the 'c' in exciting

The 'c' in *exciting* is soft and not always easy to hear, which probably explains why Danes frequently write it as exiting.

Exiting is a real word that won't set off your spellcheck, but it means departing from a place, or heading for the exits.

For example*: I'd planned to sing my most **exciting** opera numbers, but I saw the audience **exiting** before I'd even finished the first aria.*

Bragging about 'living in a hotel'

Danes love to travel and frequently tell their English-speaking friends that they will be <u>living at a hotel</u> in some exotic vacation location.

But **at bo på hotel** doesn't translate directly to English. Living at a hotel suggests a long-term residence, like an aging Hollywood actress slowly fading into the pillows while enjoying maid service.

It can also be a sad circumstance, such as when a relationship comes to an end. "Marcy kicked me out. Now I'm living in a hotel."

You *stay at a hotel* for any period of less than three months.

Mispronouncing 'prize' as 'price'

Pris in Danish can mean both the cost of something and an award for achievement, but in English, it translates to two different words: *His research cut the **price** of medicine and won him the Nobel **Prize**.*

And while many words are spelled with an "S" in British English and a "Z" in North American English — *realise* vs. *realize* — a prize is always a prize.

Differentiating the "S" and "Z" sounds in English pronunciation can be a challenge for Danes, since the voiced

"Z" does not exist in Danish. This can make *price* and *prize* sound the same when spoken aloud. If you want to minimize your accent in English, learning how to say the voiced "Z" is a great way to start.

"V" and "W" can also be a pronunciation challenge for Danes, because they sound the same in Danish but are distinctly different in English.

Many Danes overcompensate by putting in a soft "W" sound where none is required. Since "W" can sound weak and childish, the <u>Wikings</u> tend to sound much less threatening than their *Viking* counterparts.

Asking about 'bringing' a news article

As an occasional journalist, I am frequently asked by my sources when I will be *bringing* the article in a newspaper or online.

This direct translation sounds like I am bringing it to my editor in my handbag for consideration.

In English, articles are *published*, *come out* or, using the trade jargon, *run*. *When will the article run? Sometime next week, I hope.*

Not knowing 'obviously' is obnoxious

The Danish **klart** is a friendly word, suggesting that the speaker and listener agree.

But <u>obviously</u>, a common English translation, is a word with hostile undertones that suggest the listener is a moron who needs simple things explained.

If the point really is obvious, just drop the word entirely, or use the gentler *of course*.

Another unintentionally harsh statement Danes sometimes make in English is "I'm not interested."

While you can use the direct Danish translation to pleasantly suggest that you would rather see or do something else, the English phase is a sharp rejection, the sort of thing you'd say to a telephone salesman who interrupts while you are enjoying a delicious dinner.

If someone is trying to convince you to, say, attend a classical violin concert when you would prefer a monster movie, you can more kindly respond with, "I'm not really into that," or "That's not my style."

Using 'meet' to mean 'start work'

The Danish use of **møde** to indicate the time one begins work in the morning has no parallel in English.

A Danish boss who shakes hands with a new foreign hire and says "We meet at 9 every day" may get a confused look in return. "What does he mean?" thinks the foreigner. "Is there a team meeting every single morning?"

*We **start work** every day at 9* is better.

Translating 'eventuelt' as 'eventually'

Eventually is often confused with the Danish **eventuelt,** which means *potentially*.

Directly translated sentences like Pickpockets might face penalties, eventually some time in jail, reflect this misunderstanding.

Correctly used, *eventually* suggests that something is sure to happen in due time.

*If you keep picking pockets, **eventually** you will be caught and put in jail.*

Starting a sentence with 'especially'

While *especially* and *in particular* mean the same thing, it is a quirk of English that *especially* is never used to start or end a sentence.

Especially home repairs should not be attempted after drinking sounds better as ***In particular**, home repairs should not be attempted after drinking*.

The only exception is a short exclamation. ***Especially with a hammer**!*

Adding 'etc.' to every single list

The Danish writing style, like Danish culture, shies away from conflict, which is why every list of more than one or two items ends with **bl.a.** or **m.fl** as a way to avoid offending anyone by leaving their favorites off the list.

But in English, adding *etc.* to every list makes you sound as if you lack confidence in your choices — or suggests that you're too lazy to write out everything on the list.

If you want to make it clear that your list may be incomplete, one option is to start the list with *some*: "*Some of the best moments in Danish football history took place in 1986 and 1992.* "

Or you can use the word *include* — *"The heroes of Denmark's 1992 EM victory **include** Henrik Larsen and Peter Schmeichel."*

That helps avoid offending fans of, say, Brian Laudrup.

Confusing 'fun' and 'funny'

Both *fun* and *funny* are covered by **sjov** in Danish, which can make it difficult for Danes to figure out which one to use in English.

Fun lines up with general enjoyment — **Vi har moret os** translates to *We had fun*, not the often-heard We had a very funny time.

Funny refers to a humorous person or thing. *He's a **funny** comedian, and it was a very **funny** movie.*

Fun refers to an experience. *We had **fun** watching it.*

Translating 'derfor' and 'hermed' directly

Derfor is an ordinary part of Danish, but its direct English translation, therefore, is stiff and pompous. It makes you sound like a bald professor explaining chemistry.

Instead of Therefore, she loves disco dancing, try a more modern construction like *That's why she loves disco dancing*.

Just as stuffy are direct translations of **hermed**, such as hereby and herewith. These are legitimate English words that won't set off your spellcheck, but they are rarely used outside of legal contracts.

I hereby send today's presentation can be simplified to

Here's today's presentation.

Thus and hence are two more English words that sound stale and airless when used outside a formal context. It's okay in the fine print of a company's annual report to write *The product was successful. Hence, our profits doubled.* But I wouldn't use it informally: We ran out of beer. Hence, I went to Netto to buy some.

Saying 'I've tried' to describe unplanned experiences

When Danes want to show empathy with someone in trouble, they often say I've also tried that to indicate they've had the same experience. For example, I've also tried breaking my leg.

This translation of **Jeg har også prøvet** doesn't work in English unless it's something you actually made an effort to do and failed. *I've tried finding a husband, but every guy I've asked has turned me down.*

For unfortunate incidents that were unintentional, like the breaking of a leg, you can show empathy by saying *That's happened to me, too.*

Conversely, when someone else has had a positive experience, you can say that you're *happy for* them. "*I'm so happy for Mike.* He finally got a chance to run the Copenhagen Marathon."

It's not correct English, however, to say that you are happy for random objects in your own life — I'm very happy for my new running shoes. To a native speaker, this sounds like your shoes have a life apart from you that is going very well. Perhaps they are running the marathon alone.

I really like my new shoes is a more natural phrasing.

Mixing up 'customer' and 'costumer'

This mistake always surprises me, because **kunde** is a lot closer to the correct English *customer* than its perennial doppelgänger, *costumer*.

A *costumer*, folks, is a tailoring professional who sews actors into retro suits or fancy Shakespearean costumes at a theater.

I have edited entire documents in which big financial institutions discuss improving costumer service. Perhaps they see an important target group among ladies with measuring tapes draped over their shoulders and pins between their lips.

If that's not your client, use *customer*.

Confusing 'learn' with 'teach' or 'loan' with 'borrow'

At lære is flexible enough to cover both teacher and student; **jeg har lært at spille, hun har lært mig at spille**.

In English, this flexibility disappears: usage is broken into *learn* and *teach*, and they are not interchangeable. *She **taught** me to play golf. I **learned** to play golf.*

The same applies for **at låne,** which in English is split into *lend* and *borrow*. I can't borrow you my golf clubs. I can ***lend*** *you my golf clubs* or *you can **borrow** them.*

Interestingly, the direct translation *loan* works either way. *I can **loan** you twenty bucks for drinks at the clubhouse after golf,* or *you can **loan** me your clubs so we can play a few more holes.*

Using 'revert' in place of 'reply'

The English word *revert* means "return to a previous form," like a butterfly going back to its cocoon and emerging as a caterpillar. *Mike is a senior marketing manager now, but whenever he sees a hurdle he **reverts** to the boy athlete he once was.*

Many Danes, however, use *revert* in a business context in place of *reply* or *respond*. Phrases like I will revert to you next week sound odd to the person reading your email —unless the recipient is from India or Pakistan, where this construction is common.

For everyone else, *I'll **respond** next week* or *I'll **get back to you** by Friday* works better.

Thinking 'competent' is a compliment

To say someone is **kompetent** is high praise in Danish; it is faint praise in English.

Competent describes someone who can do a job, but only to its minimum requirements, and it is never a glamorous job.

You hear about ***competent** secretaries* or ***competent** plumbers*, but no one is ever a competent scientist, movie star or U.S. president. (Although a U.S. president is likely to be called *incompetent* by her political opponents.)

Skilled or *capable* are good words to compliment a worker in English. On a similar note, **kompetencer** is fine in Danish, but competencies is clumsy English: *skills* or *capabilities* sounds better.

Spelling 'lose' with a double 'o'

In English words like *balloon* and *choose* and *moose*, the oooooo sound in the middle is spelled "oo".

An intelligent Dane might then assume that the translation of **at tabe en sag** would be to loose a case. In the jungle that is English spelling, that intelligent Dane would be wrong.

*You **lose** a case,* or ***lose** an eye.* You might ***lose** weight* and find that your trousers are *loose*, a word that rhymes with *goose*.

And don't confuse *lose* with *drop*. You only *drop* something if it physically falls to the ground. You **lose** *money* in the stock market, but you **drop** *coins* all over the floor.

Annoyingly, the vowel distribution is the exact opposite for the English word *see*. It has two 'e's, yet Danes tend to spell it with one – just like the Danish **se**.

Repeating a full name throughout a text

Danish last names are famously uniform, so any group of people is likely to include a large number of Jensens, Hansens and Nielsens.

No doubt this is why Danish writers use the full name of an individual again and again throughout a long text: Kristen Jensen has just delivered 500 boxes of a brand new product. "It's the best pickled herring ever," said Kristen Jensen. If the product doesn't sell, says Kristen Jensen, it will be fed to the seals at the zoo.

This looks heavy and repetitive to a non-Danish reader,

who would expect the protagonist to be called Mr. Jensen the second time he appears in the text — or simply Jensen, or maybe just Kristen.

If you're communicating with people in the U.K., Asia and Africa, err on the side of formality and use *Mr.* or *Ms.* on second reference.

For Americans, journalistic style is to use just the person's last name. But in informal situations or with people under 30, using just the first name is fine.

Trying to schedule with week numbers

Week numbers are an efficient way to describe week-long vacation arrangements, company closures, and short-term rental periods.

Unfortunately, numbering weeks of the year is almost unknown outside of Northern Europe.

If you tell English-speaking friends elsewhere that you'll be dropping by to visit in, say, Week 18, expect a follow-up email in which they ask you what you're talking about.

Mixing up 'personal' and 'private'

Privat in Danish means things of a non-work related nature, such as a home address or a close friend.

But in English, things that belong to you alone are *personal*, like your *personal possessions* or your *personal space*. The word *private* has the flavor of something you want to conceal.

You might make a *personal* call from the office to your wife to tell her you'll be home late. Then you could sneak into the printer room and make a *private* call to your mistress, telling her where to meet you.

Using English profanity lightly

Many Danes find English profanity cute, particularly when used by small children. But to a native speaker, this language can be perceived as aggressive and upsetting. Many telephone help desk staff, for example, are trained to hang up immediately if a customer uses harsh language.

It's advisable to avoid profanity in a school or professional environment, along with anything that could be taken as an ethnic or gendered slur. Vocabulary that makes for a jolly rap song can get you in serious trouble in real life, particularly in the U.S., where a single use of a slur can end your career.

Always err on the side of sensitivity. If you're confused about the right English words to use when dealing with a highly charged topic, look up a recent article about the subject in The New York Times and use what they use.

Thinking a 'sparring partner' is a friend

When Danes want someone to join in a brainstorming session, they often seek out a *sparring partner*.

This boxing reference — a sparring partner helps a boxer train for a fight — is used to imply a friendly situation in which two equals bounce ideas around.

Yet to a native English speaker, a *sparring partner* is someone with whom you are constantly arguing, someone who needles and annoys you, a thorn in your side. Very few English speakers are looking for a sparring partner, although sometimes they are looking to get rid of one.

A *sounding board* is a more peaceful nickname for someone who assists you with creative thinking.

In other boxing metaphors, the phrase fit for fight has inexplicably taken root in Danish, although it is unknown among English speakers. *Fighting fit* can be used instead.

And if your fists connect with an unlucky opponent, he will get a **black eye**, not a blue eye.

Confusing 'effective' and 'efficient'

The Danish **effektiv**, meaning something that quickly achieves a desired result, has a parallel in English, but it is not *effective*.

It's *efficient*. An *efficient* worker gets things done fast with no fuss and without excessive use of the company's resources.

The English word *effective* is less about speed and more about impact. Someone who is *effective* may or may not be *efficient* — in fact, he may be slow or messy — but he achieves the goal he set out to achieve, and probably more.

*The **efficient** thief cleaned out every safe deposit box at the bank in under an hour. The **effective** thief opened only one box — the one with the priceless diamonds.*

Choosing 'possibility' instead of 'opportunity'

When translating **mulighed**, Danes dither between *opportunity* and *possibility* before choosing the latter.

But the words are distinctly different. An *opportunity* is always positive and it calls for personal action to take advantage of it. *You might have the **opportunity** to study in California.*

A *possibility* might be welcome or threatening, but it's usually something that's out of your control. *There is always the **possibility** that an earthquake will strike while you are studying in California.*

Both words can be replaced with *chance*. *You're lucky to have the **chance** to go to college in California, but there's always a **chance** an earthquake will strike while you are there.*

Unfortunate direct translations

"How long time until I need to oil my car?" comes from the land of unfortunate direct translations from Danish to English. (The right phrasing is: *How long until I need to oil my car?*)

Its compatriots include many money (*lots of money*), I've heard it should be warm in that city (*I've heard it's hot*), taking an education (*taking a course* or *getting a degree*) and screw up the music (*turn up* the music; to *screw up* is to make a mess of things.)

If you *screw up* on the job, you might get *fired*, one of

the two very different English translations of the Danish word **fyret**.

Fired suggests you have done something horrid and have deservedly been shown the door. By contrast, *laid off* (or *made redundant* in British English) is used when a company lets go of employees because of general business conditions.

*I was **laid off** after the Christmas rush. Bill was **fired** because he stole all the presents from underneath the company Christmas tree.*

Picking the wrong verb conjugation

Choosing the correct English verb conjugation is a lifetime struggle for Danes, since verbs do not change according to subject in Danish.

Having to remember formulations like *I **am** a swimsuit designer,* *she **is** a swimsuit designer,* *we **are** all swimsuit designers* can be stressful, particularly when the speaker is flustered or in a hurry.

But the effect of getting it wrong is bracing for an audience of native speakers, and has the effect of making you sound like a Hollywood movie villain.

Another challenge is the "ing" verb, for which there is no direct parallel in Danish. Based on context, this annoying verb form can be present, future, or a threat. *I'm in the car, **heading to the beach**. I'm **heading to the beach** next week. If you show me one more swimsuit design, **I'm heading to the beach**.*

A longer book might be able to present you with precise rules on the usage of these verbs, but this little volume can only tell you that the best teacher is experience and that using the right verb form is something you just get used to, a bit like typing on a keyboard that lacks proper Danish letters.

Using 'follow' to mean 'accompany'

While **følges ad** is a cozy thing — suggesting that you are traveling with someone you care about because you like their company or want to ensure their safety — to *follow* someone in English is much less intimate.

I'll follow you suggests that you are walking several steps behind a person who either doesn't know you're there or doesn't want you there. Expressed in English, "It was dark out. He followed her home," sounds like the opening scene of a horror movie.

As an alternative, try *He walked her home*.

Likewise, the Danish expression **skal vi følges** is unknown in English. Since it is logistically impossible for two people to follow behind each other, it sounds vaguely like a dog chasing its own tail.

Let's go together is a better option.

Playing on Danish modesty

A sign outside the bakery on my street says it sells "maybe the best raspberry tarts in town." Why not **the best** raspberry tarts? There is, after all, no objective measurement of fruit tart quality.

The answer lies both in the Danish legal system, which prohibits unprovable claims, and in Danish culture's commitment to mandatory equality.

It's all very confusing for foreigners, particularly those from more competitive societies. For them, Danish self-deprecation and modesty can come off as a lack of confidence, or even an admission of failure.

That means foreigners may misunderstand spoken jokes in which you make fun of your own faults — or theirs. In written texts intended for an international audience, it can be useful to remove waffling expressions like *it could well be* and other equivalents for **måske**, **tilsyneladende**, and **sandsynligvis**.

Similarly, while Danes go to great lengths to avoid a shameless sales pitch that reminds them of the dreaded **bilsælger**, direct sales language is perfectly okay in English.

When working abroad, feel free to say that your product is the best available and that people should buy it immediately. English speakers are accustomed to sorting through these pitches, and will decide for themselves whether or not your raspberry tart is really the tastiest in town.

Writing long and complex sentences

In Danish writing, sentences are often lengthy and as perfectly laid out as the floor plan of a house, each comma precisely where it should be. As in German, complex sentence construction is seen to represent depth of thought.

But a good English sentence — in anything but a highly academic context — is brief and direct. More than a clause or two and you will begin to sound windy.

English paragraphs are also much shorter than Danish paragraphs: Three to four short sentences are enough to expand on each main thought. Anything longer, particularly online, and you approach what Internet users call *tl;dr* — too long, didn't read.

Misplacing apostrophes

If you find yourself putting English apostrophes in the wrong place, you've got plenty of company, even among native English speakers.

Apostrophes are required when indicating possession: ***Mike's boat's*** *motor is the loudest on the lake.*

In the case of a plural possessive, the apostrophe goes on the end of the word: *His **neighbors'** motorboats are much quieter.*

Cruelly, however, these rules do not apply to the word *its*, which uses no apostrophe for the possessive. *It's* is the contraction of the words *it is*.

It's *a pity about Mike's boat.* ***Its*** *motor was smashed to pieces last night, and we have no idea who did it.*

Avoiding contractions

Danish business clients pay me to go through their texts and make them sound more natural and native. Yet they often challenge me when I replace stiff expressions like *cannot* and *will not* with contractions like *can't* and *won't*.

These clients are under the impression that contractions sound too casual, like the speech of a gum-chewing teenager instead of an educated businessperson.

The truth is that contractions are an established part of everyday English. (*Goodbye*, for example, is a shorter version of *God be with you*.)

Writers who refuse to use contractions can sound haughty and indignant, like an ill-tempered wife scolding her weak-willed husband. "Wilbur, you simply **cannot** walk any slower with those packages. I **will not** wait one more minute for you!"

Using 'already' to describe a future event

In Danish, **allerede** can be used to describe something in the future that will happen more quickly than expected.

Tærten kan allerede være færdig om fem minutter makes sense in Danish.

In English, *already* is only used in the past tense. *The pie is **already** done baking, and I have **already** eaten three pieces.* Using it to describe a future event — The pie will be finished already in five minutes — is Danglish.

As soon as is a good substitute. *Our pie company could be bankrupt **as soon as** next month.*

About the author

Kay Xander Mellish grew up in Wauwatosa, Wisconsin, and has worked as a journalist in Berlin, Hong Kong and New York. Since arriving in Denmark, she has focused on corporate communications, with staff roles at Danske Bank and Carlsberg.

She now runs KXMGroup, which helps Danish companies communicate in English.

Kay is a sought-after public speaker for both Danish and international audiences. She has delivered her "Drop Dit Danglish" seminars on polite contemporary English to schools and companies all over Denmark. You can contact Kay at via her website at Danglish.dk.

Kay is also the author of *How to Live in Denmark* and *How to Work in Denmark*.